PIPER PENELOPE PENCIL

Who has hands this small?

STEVE DRAPER

Tellwell Talent
www.tellwell.ca

ISBN
978-0-2288-5957-4 (Hardcover)
978-0-2288-5958-1 (Paperback)

This story is about a family, the Pencil family.

Mr. Pencil is the husband and father.

Mrs. Pencil is the wife and mother.

Piper Penelope Pencil is the daughter and sister.

Paulie Pencil is the son and brother.

The Pencil family always helps each other. As the story is read, stop at the end of each page and point out how one or more of the Pencil family has helped another.

Piper Penelope Pencil was sitting on the steps of the back porch doing her favorite things. First, she looked at an ant through a magnifying glass, and then she began watching a blue jay build its nest. Using her dad's old binoculars, Piper could see the blue jay place the twigs one by one to make a beautiful nest in the oak tree by the fence. Piper loved watching how things like anthills and bird nests came to exist. Dad said she was a little private investigator because she always wanted to know how things happen.

This morning, Mrs. Pencil was making breakfast. Mrs. Pencil came out on the porch and placed a bowl of grapes and plums on the patio table.

"Piper, it's such a beautiful morning. How would you like to have breakfast on the porch today?" Piper always loved being outdoors.

"Yes, Mother, I'd like that," replied Piper.

"Ok, will you please go find your Dad and Paulie and tell them that breakfast is in ten minutes? They are getting the boat ready to go fishing."

Piper laid her magnifying glass and binoculars on the patio table. Then she went around the house to tell Dad and Paulie to come and eat.

"Good morning, Piper," said Mr. Pencil and Paulie as Piper came into the garage.

"Are you sure you don't want to go fishing?" Paulie asked. "We're going to catch some big ones."

"No," said Piper, "I'm going to help Mother plant flowers."

"Paulie and I placed the potting soil in the flower garden yesterday. So, you and Mom are all set to plant the tulips," said Mr. Pencil.

"Mom is serving breakfast on the back porch. It should be ready soon," said Piper.

"Good, I'm hungry," said Paulie.

Mr. Pencil placed the fishing rods in the boat and said, "Let's go. I'm hungry too."

Piper, Paulie, and Mr. Pencil all sat down at the patio table on the porch. Mrs. Pencil came out carrying a platter loaded with eggs, bacon, toast, and jam.

"Would you please bring out the milk and juice tray, dear?" Mrs. Pencil asked Mr. Pencil.

Mr. Pencil said, "Sure, and we'll need glasses."

Paulie said, "I can help," and they went into the house.

"My goodness, everyone must have been starved," said Mrs. Pencil. "The fruit bowl is almost empty."

Piper looked and saw that only two plums and three grapes were left in the bowl.

"But Mother," said Piper, "no one ate any fruit. We all just sat down when you brought out breakfast."

"But the fruit bowl was almost full when I placed it on the table. Where did all the fruit go?" said Mrs. Pencil.

Paulie and Mr. Pencil returned with the milk, juice, and glasses. Mr. Pencil asked, "Why do you look so puzzled, dear?"

"Because I placed a full bowl of grapes and plums on the table, and now they are almost gone," replied Mrs. Pencil.

"That is puzzling," Mr. Pencil said scratching his head. "If no one ate the fruit, where could it have gone? I see Piper has her magnifying glass and binoculars. Maybe she can find a clue to tell us what happened. "

"But right now, let's eat breakfast," said Paulie. "I am starved."

After the table was cleared and the dishes were taken into the kitchen, Paulie and Mr. Pencil went fishing. Piper and Mrs. Pencil went to the shed to get out the gardening tools. Mr. Pencil and Paulie had already shoveled and raked the fresh soil into the tulip bed.

Mrs. Pencil pushed the wheelbarrow with all the tulip bulbs to be planted. Piper carried the gardening tools they would use to put the bulbs in the soil. Mrs. Pencil took the trowel and showed Piper how to prepare the bed for each tulip bulb. Mrs. Pencil carefully placed each bulb down into the freshly dug soil and gently covered each bulb by hand. Then Piper took over and started digging each spot for the bulbs.

Just as Piper was getting close to the end of the tulip bed, she noticed something curious. There in the soil was what looked like little tiny handprints.

"Mother," said Piper, "look at these!"

"What do you see?" asked Mrs. Pencil.

"Little tiny handprints!" said Piper excitedly. "Who has hands this small?"

"I don't know," said Mrs. Pencil.

Piper finished digging the holes for the tulip bulbs while thinking of the small handprints. Mrs. Pencil followed behind Piper and planted each bulb. Then Piper turned on the garden faucet to water the flower bed. Mrs. Pencil sprayed the bed with a light mist until the soil was all moist.

"Thank you for helping me, Piper," said Mrs. Pencil, "Now it's time to put the tools back in the shed."

Piper and Mrs. Pencil placed the tools in the wheelbarrow that was now empty and pushed it to the shed.

"I'll open the door and you can push the wheelbarrow inside," said Mrs. Pencil.

Piper heard a shriek and saw her mother jump. Then, something funny ran right under her feet. Piper watched as a furry streak raced across the grass and through the tulip bed. Then, it climbed right up the tree by the fence and scared the blue jay that was still busy building the nest.

Finally, the furry streak came to a stop in the fork of the oak tree.

"What was that?!" Mrs. Pencil exclaimed. Piper looked up into the oak tree.

"I'm not sure, but there it is," Piper said as she pointed upward.

From across the yard, Mrs. Pencil could not see what kind of creature had come from the shed. Piper wanted a closer look, so she slowly walked to the flower bed while Mrs. Pencil kept a watch on the furry ball in the tree fork.

"I hope it didn't damage my tulip bulbs," Mrs. Pencil said.

Piper, who was looking up into the tree, then looked down at the flower bed.

"Mother," Piper said, "there are more tiny handprints on the soil!"

Whatever the furry creature was, it was hiding in the tree. Piper peered into the tree but couldn't get a good look. Then she remembered the binoculars on the table. She carefully backed away from the tree and returned to the back porch. Using the binoculars, Piper took a look at the furry ball up close.

First, she saw a furry tail with rings around it. Piper studied
the furry ringed tail when slowly in the fork of the oak, a
face appeared. Across the eyes of the face was what looked
to be a mask. A mask like a bandit would wear. Piper smiled
behind the binoculars as she realized what the mask wearing
creature was.

"It's a raccoon," Piper called to Mrs. Pencil.

"Well, what looks like tiny handprints must be the raccoon's footprints," Mrs. Pencil said.

Piper laid the binoculars back on the table. She wanted a closer look at the tiny handprints.

Piper picked up the magnifying glass, intending to return to the flower bed, but she stopped when she noticed two tiny handprint smudges right there on the magnifying glass.

Piper closely studied the smudges on glass. *These are the same handprints that I saw in the garden*, Piper thought to herself. Now Piper knew what had happened to the grapes and plums. While Piper was telling her Father and Paulie to come to breakfast, the raccoon had spied the fruit, climbed on the patio table, and had a snack of grapes and plums. *This time*, Piper thought to herself, *the magnifying glass helped me discover how something happens and I didn't even have it in my hand!*

Later that day when Mr. Pencil and Paulie came home from their fishing expedition, everyone had a great time sharing their exciting adventures. Mr. Pencil and Paulie talked about the fish that were caught and the big ones that got away. But Mrs. Pencil and Piper Penelope Pencil had the most unusual story of the day. Piper Penelope Pencil told all about how she found out who has hands this small.